Original title:
Winter's Quiet Embrace

Copyright © 2024 Creative Arts Management OÜ
All rights reserved.

Author: Oliver Bennett
ISBN HARDBACK: 978-9916-94-596-4
ISBN PAPERBACK: 978-9916-94-597-1

A Pause in the Frozen Hour

Snowflakes tumble, heads all spun,
Frosty noses make it fun.
Penguins sneak, they trip and slide,
On banana peels they hilariously ride.

Silent nights, with whispers low,
Slippery ice, oh no, oh no!
Sipping cocoa with marshmallow cheer,
There goes the snowman—oh dear, oh dear!

The Still Choir of Winter Nights

Icicles hang like funky lights,
Singing carols with snowball fights.
Squirrels dance on branches bare,
Lost their hats in the frosty air.

Snowmen gossip about holiday cheer,
Whispered secrets that we can't hear.
Snowflakes fall with a giggly plot,
Landing on noses—yup, they're caught!

Embraced by the Frosted Silence

In the park, no one can tell,
If that statue slipped or fell.
Twirling dogs in snowflakes spin,
Chasing tails in an icy din.

Fingers freeze while making snow,
But that's nothing—much to show!
Sleds fly high, then land with a thud,
In a frosty, giggling, snowy flood.

The Quiet Dance of Snowflakes

Ballet in the air, they sway and twirl,
Each snowflake's a dancer in a chilly whirl.
Mittens lost on the frosty floor,
Wear my gloves? I'll just fall more!

Winter PJs, oh what a sight,
One sock missing, oh that's just right!
With cocoa spills all over my face,
Who needs ice skating? Look at my grace!

A Blanket of Stillness

Snowflakes dance like tiny flies,
They land on noses, oh what a surprise!
The world's a canvas, all crisp and bright,
But why is my car stuck? What a sight!

Hot cocoa spills, with marshmallows afloat,
Sipping too fast makes me start to gloat.
The snowman's winning with an old hat on,
While I'm out here slipping like a clumsy swan!

Chilling Serenity at Dusk

The sun fades out, a grand retreat,
I trip on snow, oh, what a feat!
Laughter echoes where shadows creep,
With frozen toes, I swear I'll weep.

A snowball flies, I duck and weave,
Only to find a friend, I believe.
We toss and laugh, we fall and glide,
In this chilly game, we take great pride!

The Soft Footfalls of Frost

Pitter-patter of my furry friends,
Chasing snowflakes, the fun never ends.
They slip and slide with goofy grace,
It's hard not to laugh at this wild race!

The cold air bites as we frolic around,
With winter gear, I look quite profound!
I trip on my scarf, it's too long, I fear,
Yet here I am, giggling from ear to ear!

Tranquil Twilight in White

The sky turns orange, then shades of blue,
Hot soup on the stove, I'm trying to brew.
I over-season, it might burn my throat,
Oh well, guess I'll just have toast to float!

As night rolls in with a blanket of stars,
I build a fire, forget my jars.
The flames dance wildly, who needs a show?
This is my favorite—oh, look, there's a snow!

A Lullaby of Icicles

Chilly drops hang on the eaves,
Nature's jewels make me sneeze.
Frosty air, a breath of cheer,
Brrr! I swear it's freezing here!

Sleds slide down with squeaky sounds,
Snowmen sporting funny crowns.
A snowball zooms, then takes a twist,
Oops! I hit a frosty fist!

Snowbound Reflections

Blankets white upon the ground,
Not a soul to be around.
A cat outside, it makes a leap,
And lands on snow—it's not so deep!

Ice rinks shimmer, kids prepare,
But trip and fall—oh, how they stare!
Giggles break the chilled morning air,
With marshmallows flying everywhere!

The Gentle Grace of Falling Snow

Snowflakes dance like tiny bees,
Tickling noses, oh, such tease!
The dog trots out, a fluffball bright,
Then dives right in—oh, what a sight!

Penguins slide on frozen streams,
In a world that's right from dreams.
Careful, friends, or take a spin,
You'll find the joy is tucked within!

Muffled Dreams Beneath the Icicles

Under roofs where icicles dangle,
Snowflakes whisper, twirl, and tangle.
A sled gets stuck—oops, such a plight,
While squirrels giggle at the sight!

Blankets pulled up, we laugh and sigh,
Pajamas warm, as dreams float by.
In this frosty, cozy nest,
Who knew that snow could bring such jest?

A Haven of Stillness and Snow

Flakes twirl down, they dance in flight,
My cat pounces, gives me a fright.
Chilling winds blow through the trees,
I laugh when I see him sneeze!

Snowballs launched, the kids make a mess,
Dodging them feels like an Olympic quest.
Hot cocoa's splashed on my favorite shirt,
And now it's fashion—who needs dessert?

The Touch of Frost on Windows

Frosty patterns on the glass,
My coffee's cold, guess I'll pass.
Sipping tea with mismatched socks,
Snowmen watch me in their box!

The breath of Jack nips at my nose,
I slip on ice, strike a pose!
With every slide, I yell with glee,
This clumsy ballet only suits me!

The Poetry of the Icy Breeze

The wind doth whisper, oh so sly,
With frozen fingers, I wave goodbye.
Mittens lost, just one remains,
My other hand feels all the pains!

Snowflakes tickle as they float,
Sledding down, I miss my coat.
With laughter loud, I hit the ground,
In this frosty wonderland, joy is found!

Night's Glimmer in the Snow

Stars twinkle brightly up above,
The ground below, an icy glove.
With each crunch underfoot I go,
It sounds like popcorn, oh what a show!

A snowman grins, his nose is a pipe,
He's got the moves of a dancing type!
In the light of the moon, we twirl and sway,
Making merry all through the night and day!

Under the Silver Canopy

Snowflakes dance, a clumsy dance,
They tumble down, without a chance.
Squirrels wearing hats, oh what a sight,
Sliding on ice, they take flight!

Puddles that freeze, a trap for your shoe,
With every step, you'll need a rescue crew.
Frosty breath forms clouds of cheer,
Even the snowmen chuckle here!

A Solitary Walk through Silent Streets

Footsteps crunch on fluff so white,
Wandering through the frosty night.
A cat in a scarf, sharp as a tack,
Judging my style as I shuffle back.

The lampposts wear a snowy hat,
And I trip over the neighbor's cat.
As ice turns to mud, my luck's gone sour,
But the laughter makes me feel empowered!

Soft Glimmers in the Pale Light

Stars glare down with a cheeky wink,
While I fumble, slipping on the brink.
A hot cocoa spill upon my coat,
It seems hot chocolate can't float!

Lights twinkle like they're having a ball,
While I trip on the edge of my shawl.
Each step a giggle, a slip, a slide,
In this winter wonderland, I'll take it in stride!

Hibernation of the Heart

Bears snore deep in their cozy beds,
While I sip tea and watch my threads.
Frozen fingers on a fuzzy mitt,
How many layers is too much? Just a bit!

The roads freeze over, a shiny view,
Driving here could be a fun debut.
But who needs rush? I'll stay right here,
Wrapped in laughter, winter's cheer!

A Blanket of Frosted Silence

The snowflakes dance, a merry flight,
But my nose is cold; oh, what a sight!
The squirrels wear hats, so fashionably cute,
While I'm bundled up like a frozen brute.

The world is muted, wrapped up tight,
I tripped on ice, oh what a fright!
Laughter erupts from my furry friends,
As I waddle around, my dignity bends.

The Sighs of Crystal Nights

The moon hangs low, a giant cheese,
I chase my breath; it's not a breeze!
The twinkling stars start to sway,
As I slip on ice and shout, "Hooray!"

Hot cocoa spills, a chocolaty mess,
As my mittens squish—oh, what duress!
But there's joy in this chilly spree,
With giggles and trips, all carefree.

White Veils of Solitude

The snow drapes down like a fluffy gown,
The mailman slips, oh what a clown!
I build a snowman with a lopsided grin,
Who knew a carrot could be a chin?

The silence whispers, but I must shout,
To let my neighbors know I'm out!
My dog races past, leaves me in the dust,
In this frosty fun, I simply must trust.

Frost Kisses on Sleepy Fields

The fields are frosted, a sweet delight,
I found a snowball; ready to fight!
My friend took aim, but missed my head,
And hit the cat, now she's seeing red.

We laugh and tumble in a snowy spree,
Creating chaos, oh look at me!
The blanket of white, such a clever disguise,
For all the joy wrapped up in surprise.

Calm Amongst the Winter Trees

Snowflakes dance like silly fools,
Wearing coats of white, like frozen mules.
Squirrels slip and slide with glee,
Chasing tails, oh what a spree!

Branches creak with frosty laughs,
While birds in hats take photos, snaps.
A snowman shakes his carrot nose,
Who knew he had such funny pose!

The Still Heart of an Icy Pond

The pond is frozen, a glassy sheet,
Where ducks are stuck, they can't take heat.
They quack and waddle, oh what a sight,
In their icy shoes, they wobble just right!

A fish peeks up through a chilly crust,
"Is it spring yet?" he grumbles with disgust.
Snowflakes tickle the frosty expanse,
Nature's way of making us dance!

Dreams Drifting on Cold Breezes

Cold winds whisper quaint little lies,
Tickling the noses and teary eyes.
Snowmen throw snowballs with cheer,
While kids run quick; they're full of fear!

Puffs of breath like little clouds,
Sleds crash loudly, drawing crowds.
Hot cocoa spills—uh-oh, my fate!
Laughing at life, I'm not one to hate!

The Solitude of Snow-Covered Hills

Hills wear their blankets of purest white,
Tobogganing down is pure delight!
Lucky penguins sliding by,
With a wink and a smile, they fly!

Lonely trees attempt to pose,
With icicles dangling like frozen nose.
Cold cheeks blush with snowy pride,
Shoveling paths while giggling inside!

Beneath the Blanket of Ice

The ground is a quilt, so fluffy and bright,
Squirrels in pajamas, a comical sight.
They scamper and slip, a real holiday spree,
Chasing their tails, oh let it be free!

Icicles dangle like frozen chandeliers,
While penguins in tuxes host snowball cheers.
A dance through the drifts, oh what a delight,
Who knew that a snowman could moonwalk all night?

Shadows of Solitude in the Snow

Snowflakes are flurries, a fluffy confetti,
While snowmen daydream of drinks in the jetty.
With noses of carrots, they gossip and chat,
Sharing wild tales of the cheeky old cat.

The trees wear white hats, all stylish and proud,
As children parade in their mittens and shroud.
They tumble and laugh, a mirthful brigade,
Making a snow angel with plans to invade!

The Gentle Caress of Hoarfrost

Hoarfrost is glimmering, quite a grand show,
As rabbits in scarves take a hop to and fro.
They gather for tea at a table of ice,
Discussing the flavors of snow, oh so nice!

The garden gnomes happily stand frozen in place,
While sentient snowflakes put on a brave face.
They sip from the cups that they borrowed last fall,
And giggle together, oh isn't that all?

A Symphony of White Silence

A quiet so thick, you could slice it with spoons,
While owls in top hats serenade with old tunes.
The snowdrifts are purring, a muffled delight,
As hedgehogs in slippers dance by moonlight.

The stars play their part in this cheeky charade,
As critters play poker, a wild masquerade.
With laughter and snowflakes, joy knows no end,
Every frosty adventure turns neighbor to friend.

The Quietude of the Flakes

Snowflakes giggle as they fall,
Making snowmen, standing tall.
They wear hats that flop and sway,
Perhaps they'll dance and play all day.

The sleds are racing down the hill,
Eager kids scream, 'What a thrill!'
But all around, the frost still chills,
As snowballs fly and laughter spills.

With coats so big, they can't take flight,
They tumble down, what a silly sight!
The world's a canvas, white and bright,
While squirrels scurry, quick in flight.

Yet in the hush, a silence grows,
As winter whispers soft and low.
In flakes of fun, each moment sticks,
What joy it brings, these frosty tricks.

Echoing Heartbeats Under Ice

Beneath the ice, the fish all sing,
While penguins strut their funny bling.
They waddle left, then waddly right,
In their slick suits, a comical sight.

A snowman's nose is a carrot bold,
But kids insist it's far too cold!
They chisel hard, with skill and cheer,
Creating laughs that fill the sphere.

The icicles hang like pointy things,
As birds don hats and tiny wings.
Each chirp a tweet, each flap a race,
In this frozen funny winter place.

Yet as they dance on frozen streams,
The world outside is caught in dreams.
With echoes loud and laughter bright,
Winter's chill brings delight each night.

The Enchantment of Frosted Evenings

In the glow of the evening light,
The snowflakes gather, pure and white.
They coat the rooftops like sweet icing,
While kids think sledding is quite enticing.

The cocoa's steaming, marshmallows whirled,
As giggles ripple through the chilled world.
The cat is leaping, slipping around,
On frosty ground, it hops and bounds.

The moon chuckles with a silver grin,
At toddlers donning mittens snugly pinned.
They tumble softly, a cascading show,
Amidst the flakes that swirl and flow.

And as they rush to greet the dawn,
With hats askew and gloves all drawn,
They find a magic wrapped in frost,
In evening's charm, no joy is lost.

Shadows Cast by Candlelight Snow

Candles flicker in the frosty glow,
And shadows dance with a merry show.
Outside, the snow piles high and deep,
While snuggled inside, we giggle and peep.

A snowball fight breaks out with flair,
As laughter echoes, filling the air.
But who knew mittens could also fly?
As epic fails make spirits sky-high!

The cat observes in a state of glee,
Trying to leap, but ends up on three.
As voices blend with the wintry hue,
Each moment we share feels light and new.

And when it snows, we curl up tight,
Swapping stories by candlelight.
In shadows cast, we find our cheer,
In every chuckle, the season's dear.

The Peace of Snow-Laden Branches

Snowflakes dance on every bough,
Creating hats on trees so proud.
The squirrels puff up, looking round,
In puffy jackets, they abound.

Chickadees chirp with all their might,
While snowmen blink without a fright.
The world's a stage for giggles here,
As snowballs fly without a care.

Ice on ponds, a playful tease,
Skates are on; who'll soon say cheese?
But watch your step, a slip could come,
At least you'll land with some good fun!

So gather 'round, let laughter bloom,
In nature's chilly, frosty room.
With frosty cheeks and spirits high,
We'll toast to snow till warm winds sigh.

Echoes of a Frozen Dawn

Morning sun peeks through the frost,
While slippers worn are almost lost.
Coffee brews, oh how it steams,
I dream of toast with jam and cream.

Outside, the world in white gets bright,
With snowflakes sparkling, pure delight.
Yet cats just stare with judging eyes,
As snowmen grow—oh what a prize!

Dogs leap up, they sprint with cheer,
Chasing snowflakes, they're in the clear.
Their owners follow, flailing arms,
In fluffy boots, oh what great charms!

To build a fort to fight the chill,
We load the snowballs, such a thrill.
A neighbored snowball fight ensues,
And soon, we're all in laughing blues!

Tranquil Essence of Frost

Frosty mornings come with glee,
The landscape wrapped in mystery.
But oh, those mittens stuck on tight,
A comedy of winter's plight!

Hot cocoa spills when I forget,
To take a sip, oh what a bet!
The marshmallows float like dreams,
While noses freeze in chilly beams.

In cozy homes, the pets just snooze,
While we tackle, snowy shoes.
With scarves wrapped high, we make our way,
To find the shopping spree today!

But slipping down the icy path,
I stumble and I start to laugh.
For in this frosty, funny spree,
The joy of winter is plain to see.

Gentle Clouded Slumber

As clouds roll in, a soft embrace,
They tickle roofs, a fluffy place.
Children giggle, we build a mound,
With blankets thick, we cuddle 'round.

Lights twinkle bright on trees of green,
The holiday cheer is felt unseen.
Yet still the cats will play it sly,
And jump on rooftops, oh my, my!

Eggnog spills, and laughter swells,
As family states their funny tales.
With fuzzy socks on, we glide and skate,
Who knew a pillow fight is fate?

So let us cherish chilly days,
In playful games and merry ways.
For even in the cold's embrace,
There lies a warmth we all can trace.

A Whisper Beneath the Surface

Snowflakes drop like silly hats,
As squirrels dance in comical spats.
A penguin slides with glee so bright,
While rabbits hop, oh what a sight!

Icicles hang like frozen spears,
Waving at me through winter's cheers.
I slip and slide, a graceful fall,
Yet laughter echoes, the best of all!

Hot cocoa spills, a chocolate dream,
Marshmallows bounce, they laugh and gleam.
In this frosted layer of pure delight,
Jokes float around in the chilly bite.

Every breath a puff of cheer,
Frosted fables for all to hear.
As snowmen pose with silly grins,
In this season, the fun begins!

Echoes of Solitude on Quiet Trails

Lone footsteps crunch on icy ground,
A snowball fight? No friends around!
I shout for joy, but hear a deer,
And chat with trees, they don't seem to hear.

The path ahead is blank and white,
Where shadows play with the fading light.
I trip on branches, send them flying,
Oh, nature's giggles are satisfying!

Snowflakes flutter like lost balloons,
Chasing my hat while singing tunes.
As silence hugs the hills and plains,
I swap my woes for snowball gains.

In solitude, the laughter grows,
A one-man show in winter's throes.
For every slip and slide I take,
I'll savor laughter, and snow, and cake!

Frosted Gardens, Still Beauty

In gardens dressed in frosty lace,
The vegetables wear a chilly face.
A gnome slips over in sheer surprise,
As carrots giggle, oh what a rise!

The roses sigh beneath some snow,
While sneaky bunnies put on a show.
They hop around, all full of glee,
Dressed in fluff, just like me!

Icicles dangle from every leaf,
The sound of nature's comic relief.
I speak to trees as if they'd chat,
In this stillness, a snowball spat!

Oh, frosted gardens so full of cheer,
With giggles lingering, loud and clear.
Beauty rests, yet laughter claims,
In a winter dress with silly names!

The Softness of Crystalized Shadows

Underneath the vast gray sky,
Shadows stretch out, oh my, oh my!
A snowman leans, looking quite grand,
With a top hat fashioned from someone's hand.

The ground is soft, so fluffy bright,
Footprints vanish, what a sight!
I dance with shadows, twist and shout,
As snowflakes giggle, always about.

Puffed-up cheeks and rosy flair,
I catch snowflakes without a care.
In a land where laughs comb the air,
Even the cold seems kind and rare.

Each breath I take, a frosty puff,
Yet everything is just so tough!
As I roll and tumble in pure delight,
Winter's critics laugh with all their might!

Moments Lost in a Snowy Reverie

Snowflakes dance with a clumsy flair,
Chasing each other through frosty air.
A snowman's hat sits crooked and proud,
As squirrels throw snowballs at a fluffy cloud.

The icicles glisten like pointy teeth,
While I slip on ice and land beneath.
Penguins in jackets slide down the hill,
Could they be laughing? I just got my fill!

Snow shovels clank like a bad band plays,
As neighbors complain in their best foul ways.
The sun peeks out with a wink and a grin,
"What are you doing? Let the fun begin!"

So let's twirl and stumble, let our laughter ring,
In this frosty wonderland, where joy's the king.
Lost in the dream of a chilly delight,
With snowflakes sprinkling the world, oh so bright.

The Gentle Tides of a Frozen Stream

A frozen river wears a quilt so chic,
With a fishing line hooked to a hidden mystique.
Dougie the duck takes a quack of a dive,
Only to find that the ice is alive!

Sleds come crashing like heroes on quests,
Pushing the limits of frostbite and jest.
Snow angels giggle, flapping their wings,
While a moose struts by in a pair of bling rings.

The trees start to whisper, their branches unfold,
Spilling tales of last winter, in whispers of cold.
The ice starts to crack like a silly old joke,
And giggles erupt from the nearby oak.

Let's toast with hot cocoa, and laugh till we weep,
At the silly things hidden in snowdrifts so deep.
Life's little quirks, like frost on a pine,
Remind us that chilly can surely be fine!

Winter's Echoes in a Quiet Nook

In a quiet nook where the snowflakes play,
A fox in a scarf is on holiday.
With a sneeze that echoes, he jumps in fright,
Only to find that it's dust from a kite!

The old wooden bench wears a blanket of white,
As I sit with a thermos, sipping with delight.
The snow starts to giggle, a soft little sound,
And the squirrels debate who's the best acorn found.

Frosty drinks with a splash and a spill,
As snowmen compete for the best pose to thrill.
A jolly old snowman marches at ease,
With a carrot for a nose and a sneeze that won't freeze!

So here in this nook, where laughter does flow,
Life takes its turn in this whimsical show.
Let's checklist the joy, one giggle at a time,
In the quirks of this season, forever sublime.

Feathers of Snow on Slumbering Ground

Feathers of white tilt to dance and sway,
While gnomes with sleds seem to rule today.
Bunnies brighten paths, hopping so spry,
Chasing frosty dreams as the moments fly by.

Mittens forgotten have joined the parade,
While children build castles, bright plans they have laid.
Hot cocoa spills from cups all around,
As laughter erupts from the playful, profound.

The twinkling lights fight the chilling shade,
As ice skaters twist, unafraid yet delayed.
The issue with skating? My balance, alas!
I wobble and topple, while giggles amass.

But here in the fluff, where joy seems so loud,
The season can't fail us, we're lost in the crowd.
A giggle, a tumble, it's all part of play,
In the fluffy embrace of this snowy display!

The Peaceful Art of Cold Nights

Beneath the stars, we shuffle slow,
With mittens snug, and noses aglow.
The frost bites back, it has its say,
Yet here we laugh, in a dance of sway.

Snowflakes tumble, all fluffed and spry,
Tickling our hats as they drift by.
Hot cocoa serves as our trusty shield,
Against the chill, our laughter's revealed.

Socks mismatched, oh what a sight,
Who knew igloos could feel just right?
The chilly breeze is our merry tune,
As we serenade the glow of the moon.

In hushed whispers, we trade our grace,
As snowmen sport a goofy face.
Come join the fun, let spirits ignite,
In this cold wonderland, worries take flight.

Echoes of a Snowy Dawn

The morning breaks with a frosty grin,
As we trip over boots, trying to win.
Hot tea spills in an icy swirl,
A dance of clumsiness, watch it unfurl.

Snowmen look like they're wearing a frown,
Because we've dressed them in mismatched brown.
Tiptoe past puddles, a slippery game,
Launching ourselves, oh what a shame!

The sun peeks out, what a cheeky tease,
Under its gaze, the cold's not a breeze.
Snowball wars erupt with a bright delight,
With laughter ringing through chilly daylight.

And while the world wears a silver crown,
We find the humor in falling down.
So let us skip and dodge in this cheer,
For silly antics chase away the drear.

Silent Snowfall

A sprinkle here, a sprinkle there,
Snowflakes fall without a care.
Each flurry lands with a gentle touch,
But let me tell you, they weigh quite a bunch!

Outside the window, I see swirly white,
As kids throw snowballs with all their might.
Meanwhile, I watch, snug in my chair,
Laughing at chaos, it's beyond compare.

The dog leaps high, then gets stuck quick,
Chasing his tail, oh what a trick!
A fluffy flake on his nose does land,
He shakes it off, isn't life just grand?

With cheeks aglow and noses red,
We stumble home, to rest our heads.
Here in the calm, let giggles play,
In this snowy world, we find our way.

The Hush of Frozen Nights

In the still of night, the world does freeze,
A blanket covers, as quiet as bees.
Frosty whispers, secrets they share,
Under moonlight, we bubble with care.

The icicles hang like nature's bling,
Shimmering silently, as if to sing.
But when I slip, and land on my bum,
Who knew the chill could be so dumb?

With snuggly throws and socks on our feet,
We laugh at the cold, it's quite the feat.
In the glow of the fire, our hearts are wide,
As we share hot soup, and giggles abide.

So here's to the crunch of pure white delight,
With a world so still, and spirits so bright.
In this frozen calm, may laughter increase,
For silly cold nights bring the warmest peace.

Frosted Pines

The trees wear coats of icy white,
They wink at squirrels in pure delight.
Each branch a frozen, prickly hug,
While snowflakes dance, they tug and shrug.

Crisp air brings laughter from the ground,
As frosty breath makes giggles sound.
The world is wrapped in a chilly quilt,
Even snowmen strut, as if they're built!

With every flake, a joke goes by,
The frosty sky refuses to cry.
So let's all tiptoe, just for fun,
In this snowy world, we all can run.

Sprinkled laughter, oh what a sight,
In this frosty fare, our hearts feel light.
So grab a sled, or dash for a snowball,
The chilly fun just embraces us all!

Gentle Whispers

In the hush of a morning's frosty cheer,
The trees gossip about the deer.
With whispers soft, they play and tease,
While icicles giggle in a teasing breeze.

A frosty realm of chuckles and grins,
Where laughter spins as squirrelly wins.
A snowman farts with a snowy thud,
The world erupts, it's chilly crud!

In this white wonder, mischief thrives,
As snowflakes light up our playful lives.
Each icy step, a comedic slip,
In the freeze of the day, let's take a trip.

So let's gather 'round for tales so silly,
In this cold, even the penguins get frilly.
With a wink and a nudge, let laughter rise,
In a world of frost, where giggles fly high!

A Quiet Heart Beneath the Snow

Beneath the hush of powdered sheets,
A snowman plans his frosty feats.
With carrot nose and buttons clear,
He teams with snowflakes, what a queer!

Laughter echoes in frosty air,
As penguins slide without a care.
In silent nights, the jokes still flow,
Even snowflakes giggle, tip-toe-go.

When icicles jingle then tumble down,
They whisper secrets without a frown.
With mittens on, we snowball fight,
What's better than laughter on this night?

So gather close, feel the chilly fun,
In frozen moments, our hearts have won.
Beneath the frost, let's chuckle and play,
As snowflakes twirl, we seize the day!

Night's Embrace in a Frosty Glow

In the depth of night, the stars do wink,
Moonlight sparkles, making us think.
A frosty glow upon the snow,
While snowflakes tumble, putting on a show.

As snowmen dance with silly hats,
The night giggles at wandering cats.
In every flake, a secret spun,
While laughter drips, we all have fun.

The chilly breeze whisks by with grace,
Bumping into noses, a friendly face.
In frosty air, we'll find our glee,
Running around, just you and me.

So let's embrace this snowy plight,
With twinkling eyes in soft moonlight.
For in each flake, there's joy that flows,
In this chilly world, our laughter grows!

The Murmurs of Distant Hearths

From cozy homes, soft whispers rise,
As laughter echoes under starry skies.
The smell of cookies fills the air,
While playful spirits dance without a care.

Chasing shadows in the gleaming glass,
Mittens clash as good times amass.
Outside, the snowflakes prattle loud,
While snowmen boast, all really proud!

With every snap of a frosty twig,
Comes chuckles from a dancing pig.
In this chilly world where fun takes charge,
Snowball fights grow, building large!

So gather 'round, let's share the cheer,
With joy and laughter, winter's here!
In distant hearths, the warmth remains,
Amidst the snow, where joy sustains.

Shimmering Frost Dreams

The flakes they dance in swirling flight,
A snowman grins, he's quite a sight.
With carrot nose and scarf so bright,
He might just steal my hat tonight!

The igloo's cozy, snug, and neat,
But penguins claim it's their retreat.
They throw a party, what a feat,
I'm left outside, with frozen feet!

A snowball fight ensues, hooray!
I dodge and tumble, come what may.
But fate conspired, now I must say,
I've lost my pants in snowy play!

The fire crackles, hot cocoa's near,
With marshmallows floating, oh dear!
But I spilled it all, a snowy smear,
Guess it's a frosty drink of fear!

Whispers in the Icy Air

The trees wear hats of sparkling white,
They whisper secrets on crisp nights.
I shiver, chuckle, and take flight,
I might just ski into a snowman's sight!

The rabbits hop with flair and style,
They wiggle their noses, oh so versatile.
I join their dance, it's been a while,
But now I'm stuck—can't help but smile!

The sleds are racing down the hill,
Each bump and jump gives quite a thrill.
But one bad turn, and oh what skill,
I land in snow, my cheeks now chill.

The stars are twinkling, moon alight,
With frozen laughter filling the night.
As snowflakes tumble, pure delight,
I find my mittens; it feels just right!

Stillness in the Snowbound Woods

The forest is hushed, a snowy delight,
Where squirrels wear boots, oh what a sight!
They slip and slide, try as they might,
And plan a heist for snacks tonight!

The branches groan under fluffy loads,
While I'm out here on slippery roads.
The laughter rings where mischief explodes,
As I trip over my own shoe codes!

An owl hoots laughter, perched on high,
He nods his head, I can't deny.
I wave goodbye, no need to spy,
As snowflakes tickle and quickly fly.

In this quiet time, I'll take my stand,
With cocoa in cup, I'll raise my hand.
To all the giggles across this land,
Let's toast with snow; isn't it grand?

Cold Moonlit Serenity

The moon hangs low with frosty cheer,
It shines on snowflakes, crystal clear.
I try to catch one, but oh dear,
It lands on my tongue—what a weird sphere!

The igloos shimmer, glowing bright,
While reindeer prance, what a sight!
They jest and play, full of delight,
I think they've stolen my snowball fight!

With snow angels made, I lie right back,
But wait, what's that? A penguin pack!
They slide by fast, I lose my track,
And suddenly I'm covered—it's a snowy whack!

The quiet night calls out with glee,
With laughter ringing, wild and free.
So grab your gloves, come laugh with me,
In this snowy land, it's pure jubilee!

Stillness Cradled in Snow

Snowflakes fall with a whisper,
They tickle my nose and disappear.
Sleds race down the hills with a cheer,
I crash in a pile and chug my hot beer.

The trees wear coats made of frosty lace,
I slip on an ice patch, what a disgrace!
Noses redder than Rudolph's face,
I laugh at myself, oh what a place!

Glistening ground, like a sparkly sheet,
Snowmen gossip on the chilly street.
With carrot noses and sticks for feet,
They declare winter can't be beat!

Puffy jackets make us waddle and sway,
We trip over boots, oh what a display!
But through all the cold, we laugh and play,
In this frozen wonderland, we just stay!

The Whispering Cold

The air is crisp, with whispers around,
Like secrets exchanged, not a sound!
Frosty breath makes silly clouds abound,
As we chase our hats that are lost and found.

Icicles hang like nature's sharp teeth,
I'm waiting for sunshine, to bring me relief.
Snowmen with swagger, full of belief,
Claim they're stardom, just one big thief!

Hot cocoa, sipped with marshmallow glee,
I spill some on my lap, oh look at me!
The cat dives in snow, acts strangely free,
Chasing the flakes like a ghost from the sea!

So we skate on the lake, all clumsy and spry,
With each funny fall, we can't help but cry.
With laughter and joy, we kiss goodbye,
To the chilling grumps, and envy the sky!

Shadows of a Frozen Afternoon

Sunlight dances on the frozen lake,
Shadows splat on the ground like a fake.
But then I trip, oh what a mistake,
Falling down with a loud, silly quake!

Skiing down slopes, I'm all set to glide,
But my poles betray me, what a wild ride!
I fly headfirst, nothing can be denied,
While snowflakes giggle at my awkward pride.

Chasing after snowballs tossed in the air,
I duck, but alas! I'm caught unprepared.
A face full of snow, it's only fair,
I chuckle while plotting my soft revenge scare.

In this winter sketchbook, laughter our guide,
With snow as our paper, let's put aside
The serious stuff, and let joy collide,
In shadows long cast, we cheerfully bide!

Serenity Wrapped in Flurries

Flurries fall, they twirl like a dance,
I try to catch one, what a quirk of chance!
Oh, how I stumble—no skill, just romance,
The ground holds me close in a snowy trance.

Boots are squishy—squelch! What a sound!
Each step feels like a hop off the ground.
Snowflakes land on my face, feel profound,
While robins laugh, just happy and round.

Snowballs fly in a spirited brawl,
With laughter and giggles, we spring, we fall.
I turn to my buddy, "You're not tough at all,"
But as he throws back, I'm curled in a ball!

So let's toast to the flakes that fall and sing,
In cuddly chaos, oh the joy they bring!
With snow up our noses, we dance and swing,
In this frosted haven, our hearts will cling!

Celestial Harmony in the Cold

The snowflakes dance like they're in a trance,
While penguins in parkas try to take a chance.
Their flippers flail, it's quite the sight,
As they slip and slide in the pale moonlight.

Hot cocoa spills and marshmallows fly,
Sipping too fast makes everyone sigh.
Grab your mittens, let's have some fun,
Who knew cold could spark such a pun?

The icicles hang like nature's bling,
While yetis argue who'll be the king.
Chasing snowmen down the frosty lane,
Laughing so hard, we forget the pain.

Now the toasty fire calls us back,
Time for stories and a sweet snack.
Who thought the chill could bring such cheer?
In this frozen world, laughter draws near.

Frosted Reflections at Twilight

The moon wears a hat made of fluffy snow,
While squirrels in boots put on a show.
Sliding on ice, they trip and skitter,
Who knew that winter could make them glitter?

Timmy tried to build a tower of ice,
With a carrot for a nose, he thought it was nice.
But then it collapsed, in a snowy mess,
He laughed so hard, he couldn't care less.

The stars wink down, they're in on the fun,
As snowmen argue who's the best one.
With scarves and hats all mismatched in style,
Even the chill can't steal our smile.

So raise a toast with your frosty mug,
To chilly days that give us a hug.
In the cozy glow of this frosted light,
Let's find the funny in the cold night.

When the World Holds Its Breath

The trees stand still, not a sound to be heard,
While rabbits share gossip, how absurd!
They chatter away in their fluffy coats,
Plotting a heist for some midnight oats.

The sun can't decide, does it want to come?
Peeking through clouds, getting a bit dumb.
With shadows at play, they dance on the ground,
While children giggle at the oddness found.

Snow angels flop and make silly shapes,
Like seals on the beach with their wild scrapes.
No one can tell who's having more fun,
The kids or the critters, we're all on the run.

As we pause to breathe in the frosty air,
Let's share a laugh, without a care.
For in this chill, where silence is grand,
The funny little moments are perfectly planned.

Secrets Trapped in Glacial Ribbons

The brook murmurs softly, but it's really a giggle,
As icicles jingle—a frosty riddle.
Those frozen ribbons, secrets untold,
Like a chilly diary waiting to unfold.

Bunnies in boots (yes, they're all the rage!),
Hop with great flair, they're on the stage.
But slip on a patch and they tumble with style,
Rolling in snow, laughter all the while.

Snowflakes whisper their frosty delight,
Making snowballs with all of their might.
While penguins slide down the ice-coated hill,
With belly-flops worthy of a thrill.

So let's toast to the frost with a hearty cheer,
For all the quirky fun that winter brings near.
In sweaters so cozy, we'll cuddle and play,
Finding joy in the chill on this magical day.

Glacial Moments Unfold

Frosty toes beneath the quilt,
My pet takes up my whole seat.
Socks are mismatched, style unbuilt,
I slip on ice, ouch, not so fleet.

Snowballs fly like awkward birds,
Laughter echoes, cheeks all pink.
Fallen mittens tell their words,
Hot cocoa spills as we all wink.

Icicles hanging, swords of ice,
A penguin waddles with great flair.
I ask him twice to roll the dice,
He gives a shrug, not a care.

The gust of wind hums silly notes,
An ice cream truck, but wait, it's not!
My brother's sled turns into boats,
In slush-filled puddles, we forgot!

Pinecone Dreams Under Snow

Pinecones lounge, in snow they dream,
Wishing for a warmer day.
A squirrel with a silly scheme,
Attempts to sneak some nuts away.

Snowflakes fall, like tiny pets,
Dancing in the chilly air.
I build a fort, with no regrets,
But squirrels plot—oh, life's unfair!

The dog jumps high, a furry blur,
Wearing a hat three sizes too big.
He sniffs the ground, a furry spur,
Then cuddles close, no need to dig.

Hot cocoa spills, a funny mess,
My friends and I, we laugh and sigh.
In snowy chaos, we confess,
Next year, we'll wear wings and fly!

The Sound of Silence in Snow

Hushed whispers from the frosty ground,
The world wrapped tight in cozy white.
A pizza delivery, lost and found,
Two hours late? That's quite a sight!

Snowmen stand each with a grin,
One's wearing my old, silly hat.
I wonder how they've all been,
Talking nonsense, look at that!

A frozen pond, the ice is cracked,
I'm skating on my useless shoes.
I trip again, my pride attacked,
Wishing I didn't have these blues.

The stillness sings, but here I sit,
With cotton candy dreams afloat.
The snowflakes whisper, "Don't you quit!"
But my marshmallows are in my coat!

A Tapestry of Icicles

Icicles hanging like frozen drips,
A chandelier of frosted doom.
I trip and fall, it's all eclipse,
Wrapped in snow, I swirl in gloom.

The laughter echoes, bright and loud,
As snowballs soar, they find their marks.
I build a snowman, proud and cowed,
His crooked smile just hits the sparks.

The trees wear white, their branches bend,
With twinkling lights, a festive show.
My nose is red, but that's the trend,
We dance around in sparkling snow.

With cocoa dreams and giggles bright,
We watch the sunset paint the night.
The icy world, a grand delight,
Who knew that snow could feel so right?

Chilling Whispers Beneath the Stars

Snowflakes dance in the chilly breeze,
Squirrels shiver as they search for cheese.
Blankets piled high, a fortress of fluff,
Hot cocoa's a treat, but it's never enough.

Icicles hang from the roof like teeth,
While penguins in hats plot mischief beneath.
Snowmen stand guard, with carrots for spies,
Keeping watch as the night starts to rise.

The Soft Embrace of Frozen Stillness

Pajamas in layers, we bundle up tight,
Chasing the chill with a snowball fight.
Penguins at play, they slide with great flair,
While we lose our balance and land with despair.

Fluffy the cat makes a throne out of snow,
His kingdom is grand, though it's only a floe.
Yet kings need their naps, so he curls up at ease,
Dreaming of fish in the softest of freeze.

Muffled Laughter of the Wind

The wind tells a joke to the trees in a spin,
While snowflakes can't help but chime in with a grin.
Frosty the snowman is rolling his eyes,
At kids flinging snowballs that all seem to fly.

Noses turn red as the giggles erupt,
The air smells like candy, or so we've concocted.
With laughter as warmth, we banish the chill,
As squirrels take notes in their tiny skill drill.

Beneath the Snowy Canvas

Under a blanket that's fluffy and white,
We make snow angels without any fright.
Each flake a chance to make silly shapes,
As winter paints portraits on chilly escapes.

The world is a canvas, all sparkles and glee,
With snowballs and laughter, we're wild and free.
Even the moon seems to chuckle above,
At the antics we share in the winter we love.

Calm in the Crystal Shadows

Snowflakes dance like they forgot the beat,
Icicles hang out, their fashion's neat.
Squirrels in scarves, looking quite grand,
Building snow forts with a very small band.

Penguins in jackets slide down the hill,
While snowmen debate who's got the best chill.
Hot cocoa trivia is quite the sport,
But the mugs keep diving, we need a retort!

Frogs in mittens croak songs of cheer,
While rabbits watch Netflix in their burrowed sphere.
They plan a big party with snacks galore,
Only to realize they forgot the door!

So raise a toast with a marshmallow shot,
In this frosty realm, let's all be caught.
With laughter and giggles, we'll face the cold,
In crystal shadows, let the tales unfold.

Embracing the Frosty Silence

Polar bears dancing to a frozen beat,
While penguins spin on their flippered feet.
A snowball fight with no one to fight,
The flakes just giggle and hide from the light.

The owls hoot laughter, the deer stand around,
Arguing over who's the best snow mound.
Snow angels debating who did it best,
While the frost greets us with its fluffy vest.

Hot dogs in snowmen, a quirky delight,
As rabbits debate if they're furry or light.
A snowman's lost hat starts a new trend,
While icicles try to break-fall and mend.

Sleds racing backwards with a squeaky cheer,
Even the clouds have a frostbitten sneer.
In this silent storm, we find our own voice,
And laugh at the cold, 'cause we've made our choice.

Beneath the Glistening Veil

Frosty branches wear the shiniest attire,
While the sun peeks out, a lazy liar.
The rabbits hold court, they're dressed to impress,
With carrot neckties, it's quite the mess!

Snowflakes arrive like they're late for the show,
Slicking down hills, with a hilarious flow.
Dance parties form on the icy streams,
Where ice-skating ducks fulfill their dreams.

Chickadees gossip of seeds far and wide,
While the squirrels plan heists, with nut-thieving pride.
The trees, decked in white, share whispers of glee,
Over the antics of creatures so free.

In this glittering wonder, life's a grand jest,
As critters unite for a snowball fest.
We laugh off the chill, in our crackling air,
With each little chuckle, we banish our care.

Quietude in the Frosted Air

Snow blankets soft, like a giant marshmallow,
While birds barter tales over hot cocoa mellow.
The trees clap their hands, no one understands,
What a frosted dilemma is, or how it expands!

A reindeer plays checkers with a cheeky hare,
While the snowflakes whisper of a pig with flair.
They all share the jokes of the ice-cold winter,
As sitting by fire makes everyone splinter.

Frogs in their boots leap from puddle to snow,
Creating a dance that puts on quite a show.
With snowmen in dialogue over who is the best,
And hot chocolate running as the formal guest.

We gather our giggles, cozy and tight,
In this frosted realm that feels just right.
In the hush of the season, we find our way,
Laughter in snowflakes, brightening the gray.

Silent Snowscape

The snow plops down with a fluffy thud,
The squirrels slide by in a frozen mud.
Snowmen wobble with hats slightly askew,
They look like they've partied, but just had a brew.

The kids make angels, so peace in the air,
While dogs dash by with their frosty hair.
Snowballs fly, landing with a comical splat,
Even the penguins are wondering where they're at.

Frosty breath forms in ridiculous shapes,
Like little ghosts wearing frost-tinged capes.
The night laughs softly, wrapped in the chill,
As snowflakes dance wildly, enjoying the thrill.

Embraced in the flakes, we share in the fun,
Hot cocoa's our prize when the day's finally done.
These silliness moments beneath the gray skies,
In this playful stillness, the joy never dies.

Frosted Whispers

Under frosted roofs, the gossip unfolds,
Penguins in tuxedos share secrets untold.
The owl hoots twice, then fumbles his stare,
As snowflakes conspire on seasonal air.

While chipmunks debate the best nutty snack,
A squirrel takes flight, but his landing goes whack.
His friends all chuckle, oh, what a delight,
In the hush of the evening, they giggle through night.

Pine trees with snow hats sway with the breeze,
The whispers of branches are ticklish tease.
Icicles hang like a comedy show,
As the wind tells the tales that only they know.

So winter may chill, yet laughter's the key,
In the sparkly layers, we find our spree.
Here's to frostbitten jokes and giggling flakes,
In this feathery cocoon, the laughter awakes.

The Stillness Between Snowflakes

A dance of white, oh, they twirl and they sway,
Snowflakes are cheeky, in their own frosty way.
They settle on noses, then melt with a wink,
Creating a scene that makes everyone think.

The world wears a blanket, so soft and so thick,
The trees get all cozy with their snowy stick.
In the stillness, a giggle, some crunching of feet,
The sound of a snowball, which spells out defeat.

Frosty moments whisper, with chuckles so sweet,
When kids start to tumble, oh, what a repeat!
And laughter erupts like a jovial cheer,
As snow builds up doubts on the path we hold dear.

So stop for a moment, and join in the jest,
This frosty mishap is simply the best.
In the stillness we find, all our care flies away,
In this stage of the winter, let's frolick and play.

Hushed Echoes of December

The hush of the month brings a giggle or two,
Santa has tripped, oh what clumsy shoes!
Reindeer are snickering, it's plain to see,
They roll in the snow, as jolly as can be.

The stars above shimmer, like winks from the sky,
While snowmen compete in who's tallest and spry.
Frosty hands busy with carrot-nose quirks,
Each chubby figure has its own silly perks.

Down by the river, the ducks quack in rhyme,
They're trying to figure out how to slime.
With a slip and a splash, it all turns absurd,
The giggles echo, it's simply unheard!

December's sweet moments tucked under the frost,
In this cheeky cocoon, we're never quite lost.
So raise up your mugs filled with cocoa and cheer,
In the embrace of the winter, we find laughter dear.

Milton Keynes UK
Ingram Content Group UK Ltd.
UKHW020818141124
451205UK00012B/641